AF362064

*Join my newsletter and get
my ebook library for FREE!*

INGO BLUM

Where Is My Little Dragon?

Wo ist mein kleiner Drachen?

ENGLISH/GERMAN

4

Where is Amy,
my little dragon?

Wo ist Amy, mein kleiner Drachen?

She is not in the castle.

Sie ist nicht im Schloss.

Is she guarding the princess?

Bewacht sie die Prinzessin?

No, she is not there.

Nein, dort ist sie nicht.

8

She is not in the supermarket.

Sie ist nicht im Supermarkt.

She must not want to
buy anything.

Sie möchte nichts

kaufen.

10

Is she with the
other dragons?

Ist sie bei den

anderen Drachen?

No, she is not
there either.

Nein, da ist

sie auch nicht.

Can she spit fire?

Kann sie Feuer speien?

Like in a fairy tale?

Wie in einem Märchen?

Sure she can.

Natürlich kann
sie das.

14

Is she helping a brave knight?

Hilft sie einem mutigen Ritter?

No, that is another dragon!

Nein, das ist ein anderer Drache!

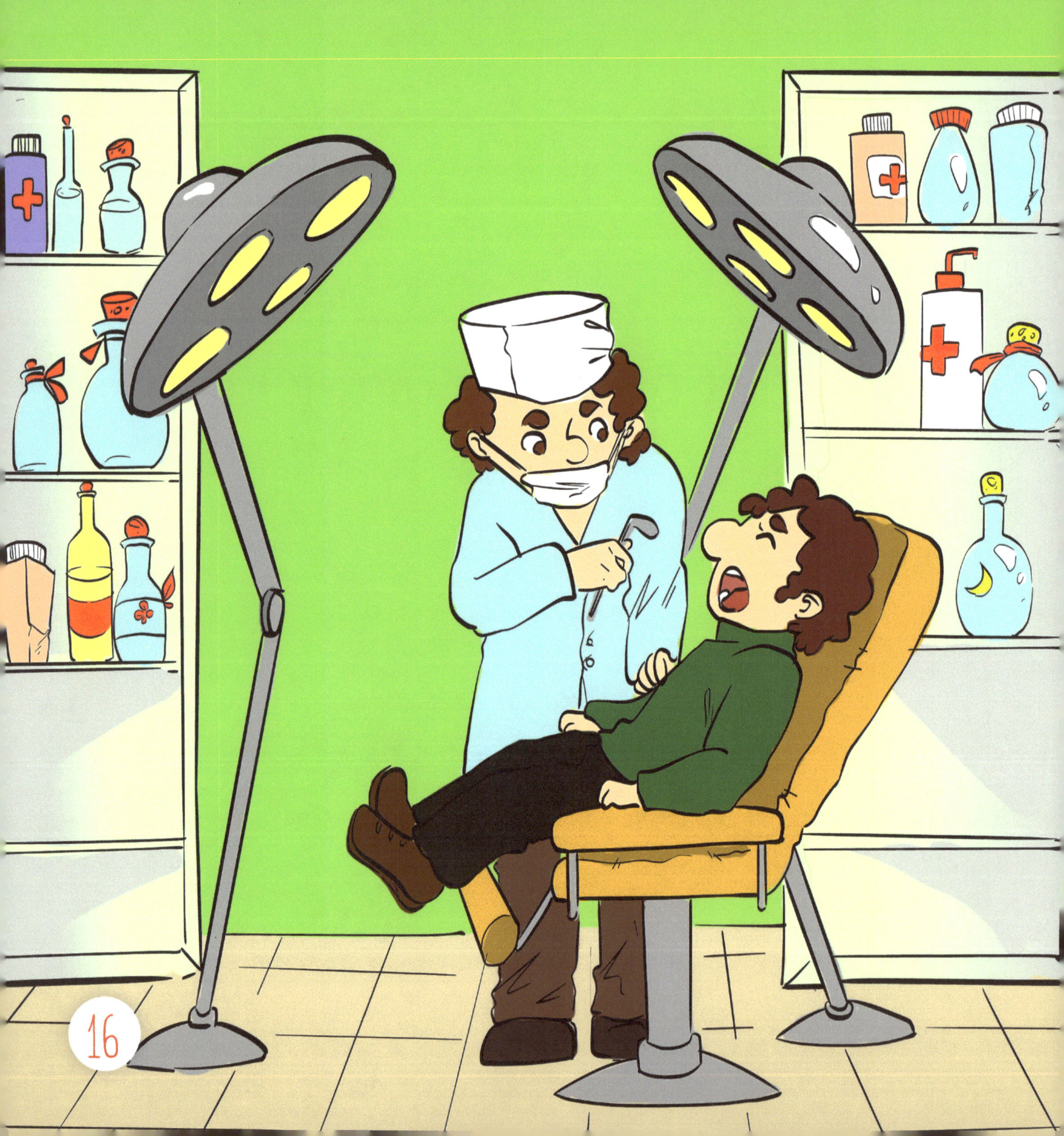

Is she at the dentist?

Ist sie beim Zahnarzt?

No, she does not have a toothache?

Nein, sie hat keine Zahnschmerzen.

She is not sick, too.

Sie ist auch nicht krank.

She is not in the attic.

Sie ist nicht auf dem Dachboden.

That is only a toy dragon on the shelf.

Das ist nur ein

Spielzeugdrachen auf

dem Regal.

Look, there she is! Hooray!

Schau, dort ist sie! Hurra!

Amy is flying through
the air.

Amy fliegt durch

die Luft.

Goodbye, Amy!

Auf Wiedersehen, Amy!

Color the dragon.

Mal den Drachen aus.

More Reading and Coloring Fun

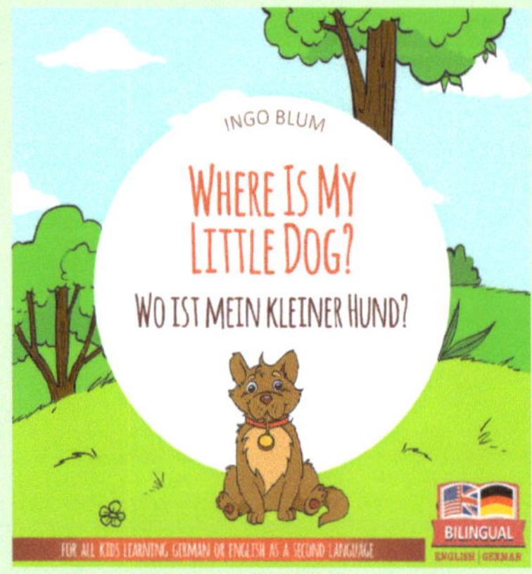

ISBN 978-1-982925-46-8

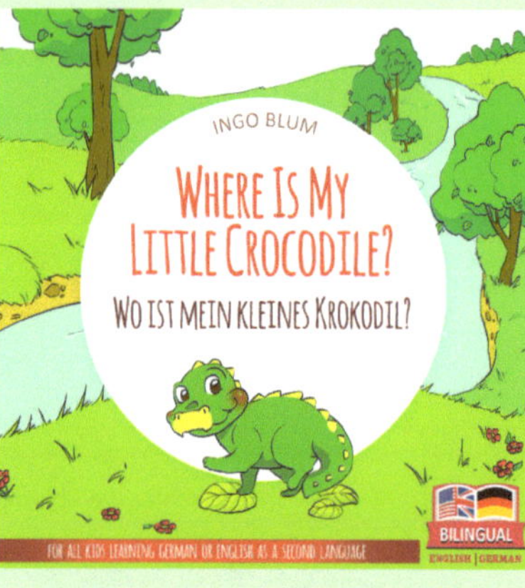

ISBN 978-1-982922-57-3

ISBN 978-1-982924-98-0

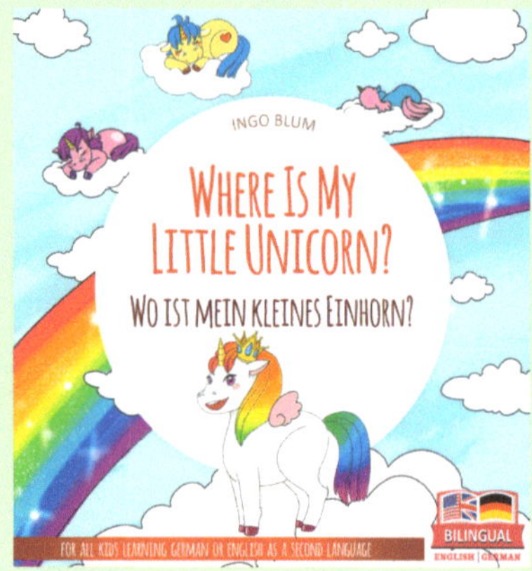

ISBN 979-8-460931-34-7

ISBN 978-1-983093-97-5

ISBN 979-8-682547-90-6

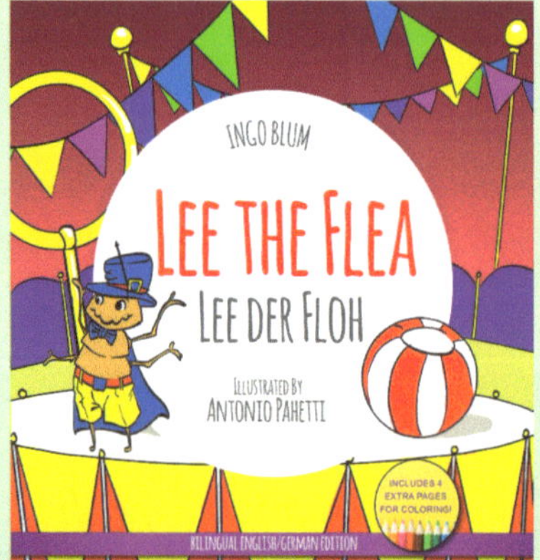

ISBN 978-1-790104-73-4

ISBN 979-8-672025-68-1

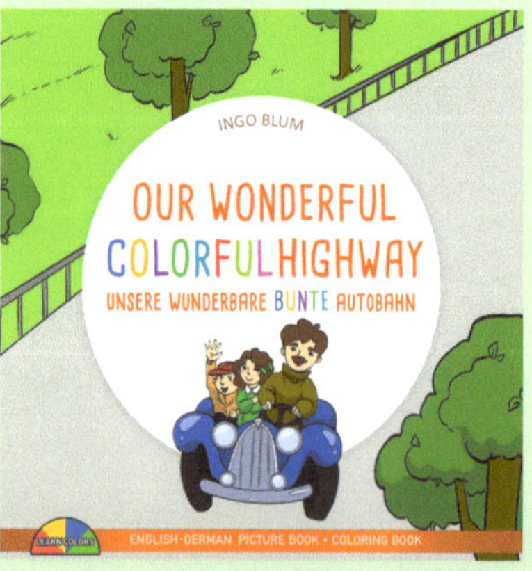

ISBN 978-1-982925-84-0